Seven Keys To A Better Life

D0816012

Other books by Dick Eastman

Love On Its Knees
The Hour that Changes the World
The University of the Word
A Celebration of Praise
No Easy Road

Seven Keys To A Better Life

Dick Eastman

Published by
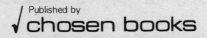
✓ chosen books

FLEMING H. REVELL COMPANY
OLD TAPPAN, NEW JERSEY

Bible verses are taken from The Living Bible, copyright ©
1971 by Tyndale House Publishers, Wheaton, Ill. Used by
permission.

Library of Congress Cataloging in Publication Data

Eastman, Dick.
    Seven keys to personal happiness / Dick Eastman.
        p.   cm.
    ISBN 0-8007-9174-6
    1. Christian life—1960- 2. Happiness—Religious
aspects—Christianity. I. Title.
BV4501.2.E25 1990
239—dc20
                                                90-45295
                                                    CIP

A Chosen Book
Copyright © 1991 by Dick Eastman

Chosen Books are published by
Fleming H. Revell Company
Old Tappan, New Jersey
Printed in the United States of America

Today is the first day of the rest of forever. How are you going to spend it? For starters, we suggest reading about Dick Eastman's seven keys to a better life on the pages following. It's about a matter of life or death. Your life or death.

—The Editors

IF I SHOULD DIE . . .

In college I jokingly told friends about my pre-exam prayer that I offered the night before each semester's finals:

> Now I lay me down to rest,
>   Tomorrow I have another test;
> If I should die before I wake,
>   That's one less test I'll have to take!

The humor of that prayer still contains an important reminder that life as we understand it ultimately ends. Or does it? The childhood prayer so many of us remember looks at the issues of death and eternity in the words

> If I should die before I wake,
>   I pray the Lord my soul to take.

But is there really a soul? And is there honestly a Lord who will take my soul? If there is, where will He take it? And what does this have to do with living a better life?

I have some suggested answers that I think you'll find interesting. I share them as a part of seven keys to a better life—both now and forever!

They include . . .

Contents

1 The Searching Key 11
2 The Father Key 18
3 The Son Key 23
4 The Spirit Key 30
5 The Truth Key 37
6 The Lordship Key 43
7 The Prayer Key 49
8 The University of the Word 55

1
The Searching Key

Hypothesis One   Sooner or later in life everyone finds himself asking three basic questions:

(1) Who am I? (2) Why am I here? and (3) Where am I going?

THE ENGINEER OF the speeding train sounded the whistle frantically to warn the two teenagers to get off the tracks. But the youths, walking boldly toward the oncoming engine, had no intention of changing their course. They had, after all, signed a suicide pact and intended to go all the way. Amazingly, lining the tracks were at least forty of their so-called friends, cheering them on loudly with shouts of "Go for it!" and "Do it!" In seconds, nineteen-year-old Bobby was gone, and his sixteen-year-old buddy, Johnny, was thrown from the tracks, critically injured and maimed for life.

Bobby's cousin Rod, a church youth leader I met in my travels, told me the story. Rod had helped conduct Bobby's funeral. According to Rod, they were just two ordinary kids looking for some meaning in life. But their search took a wrong turn and they ended up practicing Satan worship in a San Francisco area occult group. Their suicide pact, signed by eight in the group, was part of their worship.

Like Johnny and Bobby, all of humankind is searching for meaning in life. But, sadly, many end up taking a wrong turn. They're not unlike the "nowhere man" in that old Beatle ballad "making all his nowhere plans for nobody."

When this was first sung in the '60s, many in my age group were swept away by the intrigue of the hippie generation. Tune in, turn on and drop out was their creed. They thought they had arrived. Hallucinogenic drugs and free sex were rampant, and counterculture songs soon invited youths to San Francisco, the unofficial capital of this searching generation. Interestingly, Johnny and Bobby's suicide pact took place near this same city three decades later. It was just a different time and a different generation of seekers.

And today is not much different. The hippies of the '60s became the yuppies of the '80s. And as the '90s give way to a new and uncertain century, the searching continues.

Perhaps you, too, have felt its grip.

If so, you've probably discovered as I did years ago that even life's "party pleasures" provide little permanent peace. You remember the talented American actress Judy Garland. Her daughter, Liza Minnelli, who has since undergone treatment for alcoholism and apparently changed her perspective, spoke once of her famous mother. One statement from that interview left me baffled. Liza quipped, "She [Judy Garland] had a good life; she had fun. Everything was like an enormous party." As fans later learned, Miss Garland tried more than once to take her life. Of these suicide attempts Liza Minnelli said, "They were silly, halfhearted but glamorous."

The last attempt certainly lacked what I would call real glamour. It succeeded, sending the middle-aged (still young) actress to an early grave. And somehow I find little solace in the words of the existential philosopher Camus: "Suicide is prepared within the silence of the heart, as is a great work of art."

Life *can* be more than just "an enormous party" that ends in eternal emptiness. Parties alone cannot provide lasting peace. And you won't discover ultimate happiness in drug-induced "highs" or even in a bank vault full of stocks, bonds and jewels. Whether young or old, learned or unlearned, famous or little-known, wealthy or impoverished, the heart hungers for ultimate fulfillment. No matter your age or status in society, you simply cannot find peace and happiness in prestige, power or money. The latter especially lacks fulfillment. As Andrew Carnegie wrote, "Wealth lessens rather than increases human happiness. Millionaires who laugh are rare."

So I have reached a conclusion in my human experience. No matter where I travel, I notice one thing prevalent in people of all races and nations: People are searching for answers.

André Maurois, a French biographer, expressed his quest in these words: "The universe is indifferent. Who created it? Why are we here on this puny mud heap spinning in infinite space? I have not the slightest idea and I am quite convinced that no one has!"

Indeed, everyone, even the person with "everything," asks at least one of these basic questions: Who am I? Why am I here? Where am I going? We are all searching for the meaning of life. How we pursue that search is the key that helps unlock the passage to all doors leading to true value in life.

That is the reason for the insights on these pages. My goal is to help answer these questions. I will share what the Bible says concerning genuine peace and a reason for living. I will explain how you can involve yourself in the Jesus life and be changed forever. So don't stop reading now. Come along and experience this exciting life for yourself!

How Do You Feel?

Before reading what the Bible says concerning hypothesis one on the next page, check this simple questionnaire. It will take only a minute. After completing it, add up your score as explained after the questionnaire.

1. When I woke up this morning I . . .

a. ☐ found myself to be at perfect peace.

b. ☐ found I dreaded facing the day.

c. ☐ found myself wishing I were dead.

2. At this point in my life I . . .

a. ☐ definitely know my reason for being.

15

b. ☐ sometimes feel I have little direction.

c. ☐ don't really know why I am alive.

3. In looking at tomorrow I . . .

a. ☐ am thrilled with all the prospects.

b. ☐ don't think that far into the future.

c. ☐ am miserable just thinking about it.

4. In discussing life in general I . . .

a. ☐ know there is a God-given plan for me.

b. ☐ question things about God's existence.

c. ☐ absolutely don't believe in God.

Now go back and think about your choices. For each "a" checked, give yourself 25 points. For each "b" and "c," give yourself 0 points. Are you living life at one hundred percent or is it closer to zero? Let's look at what the Bible says.

The Bible Says . . .

"For I know the plans I have for you, says the Lord. They are plans for good and not for evil, to give you a future and a hope. In those days when you pray, I will listen. You will find me when you seek me, if you look for me in earnest."

Jeremiah 29:11–13

Since earliest times men have seen the earth and sky and all God made. . . . They knew about him all right, but they wouldn't admit it. . . . The result was that their foolish minds became dark and confused.

Romans 1:20–21

Let me say this, then, speaking for the Lord: Live no longer as the unsaved do, for they are blinded and confused. Their closed hearts are full of darkness; they are far away from the life of God because they have shut their minds against him, and they cannot understand his ways.

Ephesians 4:17–18

Don't let others spoil your faith and joy with their philosophies, their wrong and shallow answers built on men's thoughts and ideas, instead of on what Christ has said.

Colossians 2:8

Coming Up Next . . . Is There Really a God?

2
The
Father
Key

Hypothesis Two   There exists in the universe a God. He is the Person who created everything. He is the essence of real love. He is all-powerful and all-knowing. He is not a myth. He exists. The whole universe speaks on behalf of His existence.

AN ACCOUNT COMES to mind that happened in my early years as a youth worker. A teenager had come into my office to discuss the question of God. He called himself an agnostic and saw little reason to believe in God.

I asked pointedly, "Would you agree that the chair you are sitting in was manufactured by a chair company?" He nodded affirmatively.

"Would you further agree that this desk was built by someone who had knowledge of desk design?" He agreed without question. He also agreed that the carpet was manufactured by someone familiar with carpet weaving.

Then I questioned, "In looking at the trees and grassy hillsides, or the complexities of our human bodies, are we wrong to assume there is a supreme Designer?" He responded bluntly, "I don't think that proves anything."

What an answer! I fired back quickly, "Do you mean that the mere existence of a chair, carpet and desk is evidence to you of a human designer, yet you recognize no designer of far more complex objects?" The lad was stunned. And not long after, he changed his belief. He soon came to believe in the supreme Designer.

Where on earth did that ridiculous trend begin, anyway? I mean the idea that there is no God. It certainly couldn't have originated in common sense. Look around. Absolute logic speaks for a God. No wonder the Bible never tries to prove God; it just says He always existed.

I picked up a pamphlet recently titled *There Is No God?** It begins, "There is no God. . . . All the wonders around you are accidental. No almighty hand made a thousand billion stars. They made themselves. No power keeps them on their steady courses. The earth magnetized itself to keep the oceans from falling off toward the sun."

The message continues, "Infants teach themselves to cry when they are hungry or hurt. A small flower invented itself so that we could extract digitalis for sick hearts. The inexhaustible envelope of air—only fifty miles deep, and of exactly the right density to support human life—is just another law of physics."

Suddenly the pamphlet blares out the question, "But who invented physics? Who made the bank deposits of coal and zinc and iron and uranium inside the earth? Nobody. It was just another priceless accident."

The writer concludes, "The human heart will beat for seventy or eighty years without faltering. How does it get sufficient rest between beats? Who gave the human tongue flexibility to form words and a brain to understand them, but denied it to all the animals? It's all accidental? There is no God? That's what some people say."

And how foolish these people are. Most make their godless declarations without thinking twice. Many even change their minds in later years. History de-

* Concordia Publishing House, 3558 S. Jefferson Ave., St. Louis, MO 63118

clares that Sir Francis Newport, Voltaire, Tom Paine, David Hume, Altamont, Ethan Allen and Thomas Hobbes—all outspoken unbelievers—cried out for God's mercy in their final moments. It is inconsistent, to say the least.

So let me encourage you to reevaluate your opinion if you cannot accept the idea of God or if you are confused as to His existence. Stop for a moment and honestly consider the evidence. Be open-minded in the matter. It will be the beginning of a life-changing experience that leads to total personal peace and an eternity of health and happiness.

How Do You Feel?

Answer each question with statements of fewer than twenty words each.

1. Write your definition of God.

2. List one basic reason for believing in God.

3. According to the Bible verses on the next page, why should we believe in God?

The Bible Says . . .

Only a fool would say to himself, "There is no God." And why does he say it? Because of his wicked heart, his dark and evil deeds. His life is corroded with sin.   Psalm 53:1

The heavens are telling the glory of God; they are a marvelous display of his craftsmanship. Day and night they keep on telling about God. Without a sound or word, silent in the skies, their message reaches out to all the world.   Psalm 19:1–4

Before anything else existed, there was Christ, with God. He has always been alive and is himself God. He created everything there is—nothing exists that he didn't make.   John 1:1–3

Christ is the exact likeness of the unseen God. He existed before God made anything at all, and, in fact, Christ himself is the Creator who made everything in heaven and earth. . . . He was before all else began and it is his power that holds everything together.   Colossians 1:15–17

Coming Up Next . . .
The Truth About Jesus Christ!

3
The
Son
Key

Hypothesis Three True happiness in life, real peace and the promise of eternal life can be found only in accepting God's Son, Jesus Christ, as your personal Savior.

JESUS CHRIST! THAT name certainly is attracting attention these days. We used to hear it most often in cursing. And though people continue to use it in this way, the name *Jesus* is being voiced more than ever by people finding life and purpose in that name.

The name *Jesus* has outlived all names over the past two thousand years. In fact, Napoleon once said, "I marvel that whereas the ambitious dreams of myself, Caesar and Alexander should have vanished into thin air, a Judean peasant, Jesus, should be able to stretch His hands across the centuries and control the destinies of men and nations."

That's Jesus! He isn't just a mythical god who offers fairy tale hope. He is real. He is life. One of Christ's choice apostles said simply, "He is God's message of Life" (1 John 1:1). After receiving Him as King of my life, I began to find each day packed with the "big three" of human experience—joy, peace and power to meet daily challenges. Look at each of these for a moment.

First, Jesus provides *joy*. This inward joy can hardly be described. I can explain it only with the help of a simple story I heard recently. A father asked a child why she liked her Sunday school teacher so much. She answered, "Because her eyes twinkle like she's laughing inside all the time." Quite simply, in Jesus I keep laughing inside all the time. *Jesus is joy*.

Then, Jesus provides *peace*. Many years ago in southern Mexico, Bible translators searched for a word to use for *peace* in the Chol Indian language. The Chol language had no such word. Then the translators discovered an expression that fit perfectly. It was *a quiet heart*. These Indians don't say of Jesus that He "is our way of peace" (Ephesians 2:14). They say He "is our road to a quiet heart." And this is exactly what Jesus gives those who receive Him. *Jesus is peace.*

Last, Jesus provides *power*. A prominent New York physicist declares, "There is enough atomic energy in the body of one man to destroy the city of New York." Perhaps this is true. But let me describe a greater power. It is the tremendous power given to the follower of Christ who draws daily from God's supply house of spiritual energy. You see, *Jesus is power.*

He has power to take young people off drugs. He has power to mend broken homes. He has power to enable us to love people of all races. He has power to heal wounded humanity. And most of all, He has power to clean up the inner man.

How can we obtain this power? How do we secure this peace and joy? It all comes as part of the Jesus life. And we gain this life only by coming to Christ in prayer, asking Him to be our Savior and Lord. It's really quite simple, though many make it sound mystical or "religious." It's all just a matter of making a decision.

We are separated from God because of sin. But Jesus Christ, the perfect Son of God, willingly took the punishment for our sins on Himself when He died on the cross. "God took the sinless Christ," the Bible says, "and poured into him our sins" (2 Corinthians 5:21).

All we have to do to find this Jesus life, then, is to renounce our past and declare Christ King of our "now." This act is called repentance, which is the act of turning around and heading the other direction. We once lived in sin, having our own way about things. Now, with Christ's grace and help, we turn around. "God says he will accept and acquit us," the Bible says, "—declare us 'not guilty'—if we trust Jesus Christ to take away our sins" (Romans 3:22).

Once we have done this, Jesus saves us from a hopeless future after death (commonly called hell) and gives us eternal life (or heaven). And it happens in an instant. The Bible calls this being "born again."

Making Jesus Lord of your life is an act of self-surrender, even sacrifice, because it means you will live the rest of your life in obedience to Him. But in return, as you follow where He leads, you will experience joy and fulfillment as never before.

You can experience Jesus now! Why not stop momentarily and make your reservation for eternity? It takes only a sincere prayer of commitment. May I suggest you pray this simple prayer:

> Jesus, I come to You realizing I have sinned. You have not been the King of my life and I wish You to be. Please forgive my sins. I accept Your sacrifice for me, and now choose You as my Savior and Lord. I will live in You. It is in Your name that I ask this,
>
> Amen.

Important Suggestion: If you are serious about this prayer, please fill out the decision/response form on page 79 and mail it to the author so we can help you grow in your walk with Jesus.

How Do You Feel?

The Bible says that we can become true Christians if we confess our sins and believe in Christ as our Savior. Following are four basic steps to help you (or a friend) make this life-changing decision.

Important Note: Please check each box as a statement of faith as you read and agree with each step.

☐ **Realize** that God loves you and promises to forgive you no matter what you have done.

> I [God] have loved you . . . with an everlasting love.   Jeremiah 31:3

> We all can be saved . . . by coming to Christ, no matter who we are or what we have been like.   Romans 3:22

☐ **Recognize** that all of us have sinned and failed to obey God and thus need His forgiveness.

> Yes, all have sinned; all fall short of God's glorious ideal.   Romans 3:23

27

☐ **Repent** of all sins by confessing (agreeing with God) that Jesus Christ is the only way of salvation.

But if we confess our sins to [God], he can be depended on to forgive us and to cleanse us from every wrong. 1 John 1:9

"There is salvation in no one else [but Jesus]! Under all heaven there is no other name for men to call upon to save them."
Acts 4:12

☐ **Receive** God's gift of salvation by faith and not just by personal feelings.

Anyone who calls upon the name of the Lord will be saved.   Romans 10:13

Because of his kindness you have been saved through trusting Christ. And even trusting is not of yourselves; it too is a gift from God.   Ephesians 2:8

Signed _____

Date _____

(This is for your personal record. See page 79 to complete a decision card so you can receive further help in your growth as a follower of Jesus.)

The Bible Says . . .

And what is it that God has said? That he has given us eternal life, and that this life is in his Son [Jesus Christ]. So whoever has God's Son has life; whoever does not have his Son, does not have life.
1 John 5:11–12

When someone becomes a Christian he becomes a brand new person inside. He is not the same anymore. A new life has begun! . . . For God took the sinless Christ and poured into him our sins. Then, in exchange, he poured God's goodness into us!
2 Corinthians 5:17, 21

"When you obey me you are living in my love, just as I obey my Father and live in his love. I have told you this so that you will be filled with my joy. Yes, your cup of joy will overflow!"   John 15:10–11

"I have told you all this so that you will have peace of heart and mind. Here on earth you will have many trials and sorrows; but cheer up, for I have overcome the world."   John 16:33

Coming Up Next . . .
Our Source of Spiritual Power

4
The
Spirit
Key

Hypothesis Four The Bible clearly teaches we can be filled with the Holy Spirit, who gives us strength and power to live an overcoming life.

LET ME TAKE YOU for a moment back more than nineteen hundred and fifty years in history. It is exactly forty days after the resurrection of Christ (see Acts 1:1–14). Jesus is standing on top of a mountain ready to return to His Father in heaven. Five hundred of His disciples are standing nearby in fear, wondering how they can possibly survive without Jesus' being with them in the flesh. (Paul the apostle refers to this number of five hundred, as well as several other appearances of Christ following His resurrection in 1 Corinthians 15:6.)

Christ makes it plain, however, that He will give these five hundred followers supernatural power to be His witnesses (Acts 1:8). He tells those present that the Holy Spirit will come upon them soon. Then this Person, this Comforter and "power source," will help them tell the world about Himself. It is, in fact, by the power of the Holy Spirit that Jesus lives in our hearts (see John 14:15–21).

Our Lord further instructs the company to return to Jerusalem to wait in prayer for this power. And some do, though 380 somehow become distracted along the way. (The Bible reports that only about 120, or 24 percent, showed up for this amazing baptism of spiritual power.)

It seems, unfortunately, that we have a similar trend on our hands today. Some who accept Christ as Lord and Savior never realize how much more awaits those who are filled to overflowing with His Spirit. Many have never been told that they, too, can experience the infilling of the Holy Spirit just as Jesus' first-century disciples did. And they do not realize, further, that this same Holy Spirit can strengthen them when trials come.

It is a misperception that the Christian's life is trouble-free. The Bible tells us, in fact, that the devil will try his best to cause us misery in hopes that we will turn from God: "Be careful—watch out for attacks from Satan, your great enemy. He prowls around like a hungry, roaring lion, looking for some victim to tear apart" (1 Peter 5:8). But God is faithful and will preserve us through the power of the Holy Spirit.

How can we receive this infilling or baptism? Consider these three simple conditions.

First, *we must pray for the infilling of the Holy Spirit*. The Bible says, "Don't you realize that your heavenly Father will . . . give the Holy Spirit to those who ask for him?" (Luke 11:13). Asking, of course, is synonymous with prayer. Thus, we must specifically ask for this experience. Andrew Murray, a great missionary to southern Africa, wrote, "Men ought to seek with their whole hearts to be filled with the Spirit of God. Without being filled with the Spirit, it is utterly impossible to ever live or work as God desires." But it all begins with asking.

Next, *we must be obedient to God in order to receive this infilling of the Holy Spirit*. Scripture says, "And we are witnesses of these things, and so is the Holy Spirit, who is given by God to all who obey him" (Acts 5:32). The first command of God we must obey, of course, is to "believe on the Lord Jesus

Christ" as our Savior. Only then can we receive the infilling of the Holy Spirit.

Third, *we must have faith to receive the infilling of the Holy Spirit.* The apostle Paul penned, "All of us as Christians can have the promised Holy Spirit through this faith" (Galatians 3:14). Thus, the third basic condition is faith in the promise. We must believe that God wants to fill us with His Spirit.

What can we expect when all three of these conditions are fulfilled? Dr. Bill Bright of Campus Crusade for Christ answers, "The response to the filling of the Holy Spirit may vary from a calm assurance of power and quiet realization of greater faith in Christ and the promises of His Word to a more emotional experience." Indeed, we may suddenly sense the majesty of God as never before. A deep, intense love for Christ (and for lost souls) will come over us. In some Bible instances it even affected the recipients in a physical way. Remember, people thought the early disciples were actually drunk when they were baptized in the Spirit (see Acts 2:13). These disciples also praised God in supernaturally given languages that declared to visitors from other countries the goodness of God in their own languages (see Acts 2:6–11). It was both a worship and evangelism encounter that resulted in many conversions to Christ. By day's end, 3,000 people had received Christ as Savior (Acts 2:41).

But a feeling of ecstasy is not the primary purpose of this important indwelling. To be filled with the Spirit is not a supernatural "high" given to produce Holy Ghost goose bumps. Ultimately, the experience is to produce spiritual fruit in the life of each follower of Jesus. The apostle Paul described this fruit as "love, joy, peace, patience, kindness, goodness, faithfulness, gentleness and self-control" (Galatians 5:22–23).

I personally received this extra love gift from God one night in prayer. Suddenly I fell in love with God as never before. It was new and fresh. My heart exploded with joy as I praised God with supernatural energy. My experience reminded me of Charles Finney, the renowned revival preacher of a century ago, who said of his infilling, "I wept aloud with joy and love; and I do not know, but I should say I literally bellowed the unutterable gushings of my heart."

Of course, your experience may come differently. But I encourage you to ask God, quietly and sincerely, for this rich experience. Then, simply receive it. In fact, stay in prayer until you have a divine encounter with the Holy Spirit. And be certain not to let anyone deprive you of this promised gift. If someone discourages you from seeking this indwelling of God's Spirit, read the book of Acts in your Bible, and you will become convinced of its validity.

How Do You Feel?

We have just finished reading about the importance of being filled with the Holy Spirit and the fruit that will be produced as the result. Below is a listing of this fruit. Take a moment to write a one-sentence desire expressing how you might benefit from each fruit growing in your life. (For example, after "love" you might write, "The Holy Spirit will help me love my boss more," etc.)

1. **Love**

2. **Joy**

3. **Peace**

4. **Patience**

5. **Kindness**

6. **Goodness**

7. **Faithfulness**

8. **Gentleness**

9. **Self-Control**

Important: If you have yet to ask God for the infilling of the Holy Spirit, take time even now to pray for this vital experience.

The Bible Says . . .

"And I will give you a new heart—I will give you new and right desires—and put a new spirit within you. I will take out your stony hearts of sin and give you new hearts of love. And I will put my Spirit within you so that you will obey my laws and do whatever I command."   Ezekiel 36:26–27

"But when the Holy Spirit has come upon you, you will receive power to testify about me with great effect, to the people in Jerusalem, throughout Judea, in Samaria, and to the ends of the earth, about my death and resurrection."   Acts 1:8

But you, dear friends, must build up your lives ever more strongly upon the foundation of our holy faith, learning to pray in the power and strength of the Holy Spirit.   Jude 20

When the Holy Spirit controls our lives he will produce this kind of fruit in us: love, joy, peace, patience, kindness, goodness, faithfulness, gentleness and self-control. . . . If we are living now by the Holy Spirit's power, let us follow the Holy Spirit's leading in every part of our lives.   Galatians 5:22–23, 25

Coming Up Next . . .
Where We Can Find Real Truth

5
The
Truth
Key

Hypothesis Five The Bible is the infallible Word of God, and is thereby absolute truth for those who read it under the direction of God's Spirit.

GEORGE WASHINGTON CARVER was one of the most brilliant men who ever lived. But I consider him brilliant for much more than his mere scientific genius. Dr. Carver, in my opinion, excelled because of his love for the Bible. And this love of Scripture showed up in his work.

Take, for example, one memorable incident. For years Carver, himself a black man, encouraged the black people of the South to plant crops besides cotton. Too often a failure with the cotton crop left the people penniless.

Carver finally persuaded his people to plant peanuts. But before long they raised more peanuts than they could possibly use. So Carver sought God's assistance in the matter. It wasn't long before he discovered how to make medicines, oils, dyes, varnishes and scores of other items from the peanut.

Then one day Carver was invited to testify before a United States Senate subcommittee concerning his success with the peanut. At one point in the session he was asked, "How did you learn all these things about the peanut?"

"From an old book," came Carver's reply.

The chairman queried, "What book, Mr. Carver?"

Unashamedly the old scientist answered, "The Bible."

To this the committee chairman responded, "You mean to tell me the Bible talks about peanuts?"

"No," answered Carver, "but the Bible does tell me about the God who made the peanut. So I just asked Him to show me what to do with all His peanuts, and He did."

George Washington Carver learned a lesson we all likewise should learn. The Bible does indeed answer any question of life, but only if we are willing to read it consistently. That is the key!

So why not give yourself to a fresh and invigorating study of the Bible? Purchase a modern translation of the Bible at a local Christian bookstore and begin reading it daily. I recommend the paraphrase called The Living Bible, which is quoted here. It is published by Tyndale Publishers of Wheaton, Illinois. Good translations include the New International Version of the Bible (NIV) published by the Zondervan Corporation, Grand Rapids, Michigan; the New American Standard Bible (NASB) published by the Lockman Foundation, La Habra, California; and the New King James Version of the Bible (NKJV) published by Thomas Nelson Publishers, Nashville, Tennessee. Any good Christian bookstore will have these translations.

You may wish to mark your Bible when reading it. Enroll yourself in your own "University of the Word" and start studying for your finals. *University* means "a place of learning at the highest level" and that's exactly what the Bible is. Memorize Scripture often. If you play the guitar or are musically inclined, why not set verses to music? Write your own Bible songs. When you do this you are learning to live in God's Word. Especially important, try to read the Bible through from cover to cover each year. It's easier than you think. Please see page 61 for a practical plan to get you started.

Another meaningful way to read your Bible is to start in the first book of the New Testament, Matthew, and read a small portion, a chapter or two daily. Simply read until you come to a verse that seems to leap from the page. You will realize instinctively that this is God's promise for you for that specific day. Circle or underline the verse and write the date beside it. Stop reading at that point, insert a bookmark and begin your reading at this same verse the next day. Some days you may read an entire chapter or more before a specific verse speaks to your heart. Other days you may read only a few verses. But no matter what method you choose, I predict you will thoroughly enjoy your study of the Bible. Remember, ask the Holy Spirit for His help in understanding what the Bible says. Scripture says the Holy Spirit will guide us "into all truth" (John 16:13).

And one more thing. I encourage new followers of Jesus, whether young or old, to organize small Bible study groups at home, on the job or at school. If you are a new Christian, ask God to lead you to other followers of Jesus on your campus, on the job or in your neighborhood whom you can meet with from week to week to share God's Word and pray together. This will help you grow in the Book of Truth that God has given all His children as a standard for productive living.

How Do You Feel?

Go to the next page and read carefully the Bible verses listed there. Then write seven facts you glean from these verses about what the Bible itself has to say about the Bible. Make each statement short and to the point.

1. _____

   _____

2. _____

   _____

3. _____

   _____

4. _____

   _____

5. _____

   _____

6. _____

   _____

7. _____

   _____

The Bible Says . . .

The whole Bible was given to us by inspiration from God and is useful to teach us what is true and to make us realize what is wrong in our lives; it straightens us out and helps us do what is right.

2 Timothy 3:16

For whatever God says to us is full of living power: it is sharper than the sharpest dagger, cutting swift and deep into our innermost thoughts and desires with all their parts, exposing us for what we really are.

Hebrews 4:12

God's laws are pure, eternal, just. They are more desirable than gold. They are sweeter than honey dripping from a honeycomb. For they warn us away from harm and give success to those who obey them.

Psalm 19:9–11

"Constantly remind the people about these laws, and you yourself must think about them every day and every night so that you will be sure to obey all of them. For only then will you succeed."

Joshua 1:8

Coming Up Next . . .
The Importance of Total Commitment

6
The
Lordship
Key

Hypothesis Six Jesus Christ plainly taught, as does all of New Testament Scripture, that we must allow Christ to be total Lord of our lives in daily obedience.

FROM TIME TO TIME church attendance seems to become the social thing to do. Suddenly, churches experience a dramatic upsurge in attendance. When I was a youth leader early in my ministry, a spiritual revolution hit the streets of our nation. It soon became known as the Jesus Movement. We heard about thousands of "hippies" who suddenly left the "drug trip" to "turn on" to Jesus. Jesus freaks, they were called.

Now let me be frank. When such awakenings occur, some of these folk, perhaps more than we realize, are genuinely converted to Christ. They have honestly accepted Jesus as Lord of their lives. But some, on the other hand, have made only an *outward confession* of Christ. In reality, they have not experienced an *inward possession* by Him. He has not been made their King and Commander.

I am reminded of a veteran minister in England who was asked by an old friend how his church was getting on. During the conversation the friend asked, "How many members do you have?"

The minister replied, "About a thousand."

"And how many of them are active?" asked the friend.

To this the minister replied, "Oh, all of them are active. About two hundred are active for God and the rest are active for the devil."

How sad it is that so many new converts, and even many who are considered official church members, cannot seem to live a totally committed life! No doubt this is the reason so many church members feel so miserable. It is truly painful to walk around (spiritually) with one foot in heaven and the other in the world.

I like the way a former chaplain of the United States Senate, Peter Marshall, said it. He wrote, "We are too Christian really to enjoy sinning and too fond of sinning really to enjoy Christianity. Most of us know perfectly well what we ought to do; our trouble is that we do not want to do it."

Thus, our lesson here is simple. We must renounce our former failures—with the help of God—and walk away from them. In turn, we must become totally obedient to Jesus Christ and all He has taught. This obedience might be termed the "Lordship of Christ." It also may be referred to as discipleship or even holiness.

In what areas should we be obedient? For one thing, we should read the Bible often. This was stressed in our last chapter. Also, we should pray daily—a subject we will discuss in the next chapter. But we could also cite such necessary acts of obedience as water baptism. This is simply an outward act (to the world) showing we have been cleansed within. The Bible teaches we are to repent, or turn from sin, and be baptized. A local pastor can tell you more about this important step.

I also believe we should attend church on a regular basis if we desire to be truly obedient. The Bible tells us not to neglect our fellowship with other believers (Hebrews 10:24–25). Ask the Lord today to lead you to a good church if you have yet to find one.

To make Jesus Lord, we must also obey Him in telling others about what He has done for us. Followers of Jesus often refer to this as "witnessing" for our Lord (see Acts 1:8).

This entire subject of the Lordship of Christ, or discipleship, might be termed *continuance*. This means that after we receive Christ as Savior we do not stop there. Rather, we allow Him daily to be Lord of all our decisions. And just how do we gain strength for this? We certainly cannot find it in ourselves. It comes from above.

Let me illustrate with a lesson from nature. Have you ever gazed upon a giant redwood? I have sat beneath the California redwood trees that reach heights of 360 feet. How do they draw water to their leaves? Botanists tell us this process is not accomplished by pressure from the roots below. Rather, it is done by the pull of the atmosphere above.

So it is for those who wish to grow in Jesus. *To grow taller, we must reach higher*. Jesus will pull you from above. He is your strength. *In Christ we grow*. And prayer, as we'll soon discover, is the key to nurturing this growth.

How Do You Feel?

Read the Scriptures carefully on the next page. Underline key phrases about what it means to make Jesus Lord of your life. Then fill in the blanks below (based on these verses).

1. To make Jesus Lord, my heart must be_____
   _____ toward God so He can show His great
   _____ in helping me serve Him (2
   Chronicles 16:9).
2. To make Jesus Lord I must not become tied up
   in _____ affairs, for that would not satisfy the one who has enlisted me in His army (2
   Timothy 2:3–4).
3. To make Jesus Lord, I need to use God's mighty
   _____ to _____ down the dev-
   il's strongholds (2 Corinthians 10:3–4).
4. To make Jesus Lord, I need to turn away from
   everything _____, whether in body or
   spirit, and _____ myself, so I can give
   myself to Him alone (2 Corinthians 7:1).

The Bible Says . . .

For the eyes of the Lord search back and forth
across the whole earth, looking for people whose
hearts are perfect toward him, so that he can show
his great power in helping them.

2 Chronicles 16:9

Take your share of suffering as a good soldier of
Jesus Christ, just as I do, and as Christ's soldier do
not let yourself become tied up in worldly affairs, for
then you cannot satisfy the one who has enlisted you
in his army. 2 Timothy 2:3–4

It is true that I am an ordinary, weak human being, but I don't use human plans and methods to win

my battles. I use God's mighty weapons, not those made by men, to knock down the devil's strongholds.

2 Corinthians 10:3–4

Having such great promises as these, dear friends, let us turn away from everything wrong, whether of body or spirit, and purify ourselves, living in the wholesome fear of God, giving ourselves to him alone.

2 Corinthians 7:1

Coming Up Next . . .
How to Communicate with God

7
The
Prayer
Key

Hypothesis Seven   It is a Bible premise that God will hear the prayers Christians pray and, further, that daily prayer is essential if we wish to survive spiritually.

WE COME NOW to a crucial part of our time together. It concerns communication with God Himself. This is called prayer. And prayer works. Dwight Eisenhower, one of America's great presidents, said, "Prayer gives you the courage to make the decisions you must make in a crisis and then the confidence to leave the results to a higher power."

As you press forward in your Christian experience, you will sometimes collide with problems that seem insurmountable. You will need outside help to get you through. Where do you gain this help? From God, through prayer. That's because prayer accesses power. Prayer links us with our powerful Creator. I like the description a great scientist gives: "Prayer is the mightiest force in the universe."

There are, of course, several conditions that make prayer effective. These conditions are important to understand if we desire answers to our prayers. Please examine these with me a moment.

First, we must not allow sin in our lives. Sin hinders prayer. In Psalms the writer says, "I cried to him [God] for help, with praises ready on my tongue. He would not have listened if I had not confessed my sins" (Psalm 66:17–18). Here we discover that we must not allow sin in our lives if we wish to have our prayers answered. Confession of all known sins opens the gateway to God.

Second, we must use the name of Jesus as our basis for effective prayer. Quite simply, we are asking God to answer each prayer with the name of His Son standing behind all that we pray. Jesus Himself said, "Yes, ask *anything,* using my name, and I will do it!" (John 14:14).

Third, we must decide before we pray to let God do as He desires concerning the things for which we pray. This is generally referred to as "seeking God's will." Those who pray must learn the necessity of letting God answer their prayers as He sees fit. Sometimes we may find ourselves waiting at great length for an answer. This is often necessary because God sees the wait as needful. Perhaps He wants us to seek Him more than just seeking answers to our prayers. The Bible says, "We are sure of this, that he will listen to us whenever we ask him for anything *in line with his will*" (1 John 5:14). And His will is, first of all, that we know Him better.

Never forget these important factors in prayer. We must confess our sins and come to God with a clean heart. We must pray in the name of Jesus. And we must desire God's will in each instance, no matter what we may wish personally.

What else can be said concerning prayer? Perhaps I should mention that God answers prayer in three basic ways. He may say *yes* or *no* or *wait.* Thus, the most important thing we can do in prayer is let God be God and reserve for Him the right to choose what He wishes concerning a particular prayer.

How might you develop a daily time of prayer? Here are three suggestions that will help you spend at least fifteen minutes a day in prayer. I call them the three "musts" for a meaningful prayer time. (For ideas on how to spend as much as an hour in prayer each day, plus a 31-day prayer guide for personal growth, see pages 72–77).

First, I must touch the Lord in prayer. This concerns praise, thanksgiving and worship. Tell God why you love Him and thank Him for every blessing you can think of. Praise Him for who He is. Take at least five minutes to do this.

Second, I must touch His Word in prayer. Remember all we said earlier about Bible reading? Here's your chance to hear from God. Take another five minutes (or more) for this aspect of prayer.

Third, I must touch my world in prayer. This is a time to pray for others. (The ministry I direct, Every Home for Christ, prints an annual World Prayer Map to help you pray for your world every day.) Most important, make your time with Jesus the key to your day.

It is also important to remember that age is not important in determining one's effectiveness in prayer. Both King Uzziah and King Josiah were only sixteen years old when the Bible says they sought after God. (See 2 Chronicles 26 and 34). Anna, on the other hand, was 84 years of age when she served as a full-time prayer warrior (Luke 2:36–37).

How Do You Feel?

David Livingstone, the great African missionary, had the habit of writing a special prayer once each year on his birthday for the following year. Write a

prayer to God today and list your desires for the next
twelve months.

Dear God,

Signed_____

Date_____

The Bible Says . . .

Pray all the time. Ask God for anything in line with the Holy Spirit's wishes. Plead with him, reminding him of your needs, and keep praying earnestly for all Christians everywhere.

Ephesians 6:18

Pray much for others; plead for God's mercy upon them; give thanks for all he is going to do for them. Pray in this way for kings and all others who are in authority over us, or are in places of high responsibility, so that we can live in peace and quietness, spending our time in godly living and thinking much about the Lord.   1 Timothy 2:1–2

"Listen to me! You can pray for anything, and if you believe, you have it; it's yours! But when you are praying, first forgive anyone you are holding a grudge against, so that your Father in heaven will forgive you your sins too."   Mark 11:24–25

"Ask, and you will be given what you ask for. Seek, and you will find. Knock, and the door will be opened. For everyone who asks, receives. Anyone who seeks, finds. If only you will knock, the door will open."   Matthew 7:7–8

8
The University of the Word

Note: If you wish you may remove pages 55–77 to keep in your Bible.

Seven Keys to a Better Life

WELCOME TO THE University of the Word. Let me encourage you to enroll in this course, starting today. There is only one primary textbook, the Bible. And though you may read other good Christian literature (and should!), the Bible must remain your key source of nurture.

In the 52-week plan you are to read, study, analyze and digest each assigned chapter for a particular week. Read the chapter through completely during the first two days of that week. Then reread it several verses at a time, taking notes. Note key words in each verse and do a word study. If you wish, write poetry based on one verse or two of that chapter. Or, if you are musically inclined, compose music for a portion of the chapter. Also, try to memorize at least one verse from that chapter.

You have seven full days to accomplish each weekly assignment. It will take much self-discipline, and you will have to grade yourself. Put a check before each assigned chapter when you have completed that week's assignment. If you do not have a Bible, I recommend any of the versions mentioned in chapter 5. No matter the translation, the important thing is to start at once.

Here is the 52-week plan, followed by a day-by-day Bible study guide.

56

52-Week Plan

Check when completed. Study a chapter each week.

☐ 1. Study Matthew 5
Important Teachings of Jesus

☐ 2. Study Mark 16
Christ's final instructions to disciples

☐ 3. Study Luke 10
More instructions from Jesus

☐ 4. Study John 15
Living in Jesus

☐ 5. Study Acts 2
Early Church patterns for power

☐ 6. Study Romans 8
Walking in God's Spirit

☐ 7. Study 1 Corinthians 13
The love chapter

☐ 8. Study 2 Corinthians 12
Growing in grace

☐ 9. Study Galatians 5
The fruit of the Spirit

☐ 10. Study Ephesians 6
God's armor for battle

☐ 11. Study Philippians 4
A study of the pure life

☐ 12. Study Colossians 3
Things to seek in life

☐ 13. Study 1 Thessalonians 5
Between now and Christ's coming

Seven Keys to a Better Life

☐ 14. Study 2 Thessalonians 2
   About the day of the Lord

☐ 15. Study 1 Timothy 6
   Learning to be content

☐ 16. Study 2 Timothy 2
   Developing as Jesus' soldier

☐ 17. Study Titus 3
   Lessons in Christ's grace and mercy

☐ 18. Study Philemon (25 verses)
   Love of master to servant

☐ 19. Study Hebrews 11
   Lessons in faith

☐ 20. Study James 2
   Faith and works combined

☐ 21. Study 1 Peter 2
   Growing in God's Word

☐ 22. Study 2 Peter 1
   Lessons in spiritual addition

☐ 23. Study 1 John 4
   Lessons in love

☐ 24. Study 2 John (13 verses)
   Rejecting false doctrine

☐ 25. Study 3 John (15 verses)
   Soul prosperity

☐ 26. Study Jude (25 verses)
   Contending for the faith

☐ 27. Study Revelation 21
   Our future home in heaven

☐ 28. Study Genesis 3
   First temptation and sin

☐ 29. Study Exodus 20
The Ten Commandments

☐ 30. Study Leviticus 26
"If" clauses for God's blessings

☐ 31. Study Numbers 13
The positive vs. the negative

☐ 32. Study Numbers 21
Time to move forward

☐ 33. Study Joshua 3
God will do wonders

☐ 34. Study Judges 6
The story of Gideon

☐ 35. Study 1 Samuel 15
The need for obedience

☐ 36. Study 2 Samuel 12
We reap what is sowed

☐ 37. Study 1 Kings 19
The quiet voice of God

☐ 38. Study 2 Kings 2
The double portion of the Spirit

☐ 39. Study 1 Chronicles 14
God prepares a miracle army

☐ 40. Study 2 Chronicles 5
The glory in the Temple

☐ 41. Study Ezra 10
A pledge to real holiness

☐ 42. Study Nehemiah 2
Let us build for God

☐ 43. Study Job 1
A lesson in amazing faith

Seven Keys to a Better Life

- [ ] 44. Study Psalm 119
  The truth about the truth

- [ ] 45. Study Proverbs 3
  Trusting God and His Word

- [ ] 46. Study Isaiah 62
  Here come "the holy people"

- [ ] 47. Study Jeremiah 1
  Lessons in courage

- [ ] 48. Study Lamentations 3
  Lessons in God's compassion

- [ ] 49. Study Ezekiel 37
  An army on the rise

- [ ] 50. Study Daniel 6
  A look at a prayer habit

- [ ] 51. Study Joel 2
  Some things to come

- [ ] 52. Study Malachi 3
  Lessons on giving

NOTE: When you have completed this basic overview of the Bible, begin a systematic study of the entire Bible— book by book, chapter by chapter. It will revolutionize your life. After doing the above study use the following day-by-day Bible study guide for reading the Bible through in one year. This can be done simultaneously with the above study, or in your second year enrolled in The University of the Word.

Daily Guide

January

☐ 1 Ps. 1–2; Gen. 1–2; Mt. 1–3

☐ 2 Ps. 3; Gen. 3–4; Mt. 4

☐ 3 Ps. 4; Gen. 5–6; Mt. 5

☐ 4 Ps. 5; Gen. 7–8; Mt. 6

☐ 5 Ps. 6; Gen. 9–10; Mt. 7–8

☐ 6 Ps. 7; Gen. 11–12; Mt. 9–11

☐ 7 Ps. 8; Gen. 13–14; Mt. 12

☐ 8 Ps. 9–10; Gen. 15–16; Mt. 13

☐ 9 Ps. 11; Gen. 17–18; Mt. 14

☐ 10 Ps. 12; Gen. 19–20; Mt. 15–16

☐ 11 Ps. 13; Gen. 21–22; Mt. 17

☐ 12 Ps. 14; Gen. 23–24; Mt. 18–20

☐ 13 Ps. 15; Gen. 25–26; Mt. 21

☐ 14 Ps. 16; Gen. 27–28; Mt. 22

☐ 15 Ps. 17–18; Gen. 29–30; Mt. 23

☐ 16 Ps. 19; Gen. 31–32; Mt. 24–25

☐ 17 Ps. 20; Gen. 33–34; Mt. 26

☐ 18 Ps. 21; Gen. 35–36; Mt. 27–28

☐ 19 Ps. 22; Gen. 37–38; Mk. 1–2

☐ 20 Ps. 23; Gen. 39–40; Mk. 3

☐ 21 Ps. 24; Gen. 41–42; Mk. 4

☐ 22 Ps. 25–26; Gen. 43–44; Mk. 5

☐ 23 Ps. 27; Gen. 45–46; Mk. 6–7

☐ 24 Ps. 28; Gen. 47–48; Mk. 8–10

☐ 25 Ps. 29; Gen. 49–50; Mk. 11

☐ 26 Ps. 30; Ex. 1–2; Mk. 12

☐ 27 Ps. 31; Ex. 3–4; Mk. 13

☐ 28 Ps. 32; Ex. 5–6; Mk. 14

☐ 29 Ps. 33–34; Ex. 7–8; Mk. 15

☐ 30 Ps. 35; Ex. 9–10; Mk. 16

☐ 31 Ps. 36; Ex. 11–12; Lk. 1–3

February

☐ 1 Ps. 37; Ex. 13–14; Lk. 4–5

☐ 2 Ps. 38; Ex. 15–16; Lk. 6

☐ 3 Ps. 39; Ex. 17–18; Lk. 7

☐ 4 Ps. 40; Ex. 19–20; Lk. 8

☐ 5 Ps. 41–42; Ex. 21–22; Lk. 9

☐ 6 Ps. 43; Ex. 23–24; Lk. 10–12

☐ 7 Ps. 44; Ex. 25–26; Lk. 13

☐ 8 Ps. 45; Ex. 27–28; Lk. 14–15

☐ 9 Ps. 46; Ex. 29–30; Lk. 16–17

☐ 10 Ps. 47; Ex. 31–32; Lk. 18

☐ 11 Ps. 48; Ex. 33–34; Lk. 19–21

☐ 12 Ps. 49–50; Ex. 35–36; Lk. 22

☐ 13 Ps. 51; Ex. 37–38; Lk. 23

☐ 14 Ps. 52; Ex. 39–40; Lk. 24

☐ 15 Ps. 53; Lev. 1–2; Jn. 1–2

☐ 16 Ps. 54; Lev. 3–4; Jn. 3

☐ 17 Ps. 55; Lev. 5–6; Jn. 4–6

☐ 18 Ps. 56; Lev. 7–8; Jn. 7

☐ 19 Ps. 57–58; Lev. 9–10; Jn. 8

☐ 20 Ps. 59; Lev. 11–12; Jn. 9

☐ 21 Ps. 60; Lev. 13–14; Jn. 10

☐ 22 Ps. 61; Lev. 15–16; Jn. 11

☐ 23 Ps. 62; Lev. 17–18; Jn. 12

☐ 24 Ps. 63; Lev. 19–20; Jn. 13–15

☐ 25 Ps. 64; Lev. 21–22; Jn. 16–17

☐ 26 Ps. 65–66; Lev. 23–24; Jn. 18

☐ 27 Ps. 67; Lev. 25–26; Jn. 19

☐ 28 Ps. 68; Lev. 27; Jn. 20

March

☐ 1 Ps. 69; Num. 1–3; Jn. 21

☐ 2 Ps. 70; Num. 4–5; Acts 1–3

☐ 3 Ps. 71; Num. 6–7; Acts 4

☐ 4 Ps. 72; Num. 8–9; Acts 5

☐ 5 Ps. 73–74; Num. 10–11; Acts 6

☐ 6 Ps. 75; Num. 12–13; Acts 7–8

☐ 7 Ps. 76; Num. 14–15; Acts 9

☐ 8 Ps. 77; Num. 16–17; Acts 10–12

☐ 9 Ps. 78; Num. 18–19; Acts 13

☐ 10 Ps. 79; Num. 20–21; Acts 14

☐ 11 Ps. 80–81; Num. 22–23; Acts 15

☐ 12 Ps. 82; Num. 24–25; Acts 16

☐ 13 Ps. 83; Num. 26–27; Acts 17

☐ 14 Ps. 84; Num. 28–29; Acts 18

☐ 15 Ps. 85; Num. 30–31; Acts 19–21

☐ 16 Ps. 86; Num. 32–33; Acts 22

☐ 17 Ps. 87; Num. 34–35; Acts 23

☐ 18 Ps. 88; Num. 36; Acts 24

☐ 19 Ps. 89; Deut. 1–3; Acts 25

☐ 20 Ps. 90; Deut. 4–5; Acts 26–27

☐ 21 Ps. 91; Deut. 6–7; Acts 28

☐ 22 Ps. 92; Deut. 8–9; Rom. 1–3

☐ 23 Ps. 93; Deut. 10–11; Rom. 4

☐ 24 Ps. 94; Deut. 12–13; Rom. 5

☐ 25 Ps. 95; Deut. 14–15; Rom. 6–7

☐ 26 Ps. 96–97; Deut. 16–17; Rom. 8

☐ 27 Ps. 98; Deut. 18–19; Rom. 9–10

☐ 28 Ps. 99; Deut. 20–21; Rom. 11

☐ 29 Ps. 100; Deut. 22–23; Rom. 12–13

☐ 30 Ps. 101; Deut. 24–25; Rom. 14

☐ 31 Ps. 102; Deut. 26–27; Rom. 15–16

April

☐ 1 Ps. 103–104; Deut. 28–29; 1 Cor. 1

☐ 2 Ps. 105; Deut. 30–31; 1 Cor. 2–4

☐ 3 Ps. 106; Deut. 32–33; 1 Cor. 5

☐ 4 Ps. 107; Deut. 34; 1 Cor. 6

☐ 5 Ps. 108; Josh. 1–3; 1 Cor. 7

☐ 6 Ps. 109; Josh. 4–5; 1 Cor. 8–9

☐ 7 Ps. 110; Josh. 6–7; 1 Cor. 10

☐ 8 Ps. 111; Josh. 8–9; 1 Cor. 11–13

☐ 9 Ps. 112; Josh. 10–11; 1 Cor. 14

☐ 10 Ps. 113–114; Josh. 12–13; 1 Cor. 15

☐ 11 Ps. 115; Josh. 14–15; 1 Cor. 16

☐ 12 Ps. 116; Josh. 16–17; 2 Cor. 1

☐ 13 Ps. 117; Josh. 18–19; 2 Cor. 2–3

☐ 14 Ps. 118; Josh. 20–21; 2 Cor. 4–6

☐ 15 Ps. 119:1–48; Josh. 22–23; 2 Cor. 7

Seven Keys to a Better Life

- [ ] 16 Ps. 119:49–80;
       Josh. 24; 2 Cor. 8
- [ ] 17 Ps. 119:81–96;
       Jud. 1–3; 2 Cor. 9
- [ ] 18 Ps. 119:97–128;
       Jud. 4–5; 2 Cor.
       10
- [ ] 19 Ps. 119:129–144;
       Jud. 6–7; 2 Cor.
       11
- [ ] 20 Ps. 119:145–176;
       Jud. 8–9; 2 Cor.
       12–13
- [ ] 21 Ps. 120; Jud.
       10–11; Gal. 1–3
- [ ] 22 Ps. 121; Jud.
       12–13; Gal. 4
- [ ] 23 Ps. 122; Jud.
       14–15; Gal. 5
- [ ] 24 Ps. 123; Jud.
       16–17; Gal. 6
- [ ] 25 Ps. 124; Jud.
       18–19; Eph. 1
- [ ] 26 Ps. 125; Jud.
       20–21; Eph. 2
- [ ] 27 Ps. 126; Ruth
       1–2; Eph. 3–5
- [ ] 28 Ps. 127; Ruth
       3–4; Eph. 6
- [ ] 29 Ps. 128; 1 Sam.
       1–2; Phil. 1
- [ ] 30 Ps. 129–130; 1
       Sam. 3–4; Phil.
       2–3

May

- [ ] 1 Ps. 131–132; 1
      Sam. 5–6; Phil. 4

- [ ] 2 Ps. 133; 1 Sam.
      7–8; Col. 1
- [ ] 3 Ps. 134; 1 Sam.
      9–10; Col. 2–4
- [ ] 4 Ps. 135; 1 Sam.
      11–12; 1 Thess. 1
- [ ] 5 Ps. 136; 1 Sam.
      13–14; 1 Thess.
      2–3
- [ ] 6 Ps. 137; 1 Sam.
      15–16; 1 Thess. 4
- [ ] 7 Ps. 138; 1 Sam.
      17–18; 1 Thess. 5
- [ ] 8 Ps. 139; 1 Sam.
      19–20; 2 Thess. 1
- [ ] 9 Ps. 140; 1 Sam.
      21–22; 2 Thess.
      2–3
- [ ] 10 Ps. 141; 1 Sam.
       23–24; 1 Tim.
       1–2
- [ ] 11 Ps. 142; 1 Sam.
       25–26; 1 Tim. 3
- [ ] 12 Ps. 143; 1 Sam.
       27–28; 1 Tim. 4
- [ ] 13 Ps. 144; 1 Sam.
       29–30; 1 Tim.
       5–6
- [ ] 14 Ps. 145–146; 1
       Sam. 31; 2 Tim.
       1–2
- [ ] 15 Ps. 147; 2 Sam.
       1–3; 2 Tim. 3–4
- [ ] 16 Ps. 148; 2 Sam.
       4–5; Titus 1
- [ ] 17 Ps. 149; 2 Sam.
       6–7; Titus 2–3

- [ ] 18 Ps. 150; 2 Sam. 8–9; Philemon
- [ ] 19 Prov. 1; 2 Sam. 10–11; Heb. 1
- [ ] 20 Prov. 2; 2 Sam. 12–13; Heb. 2
- [ ] 21 Prov. 3–4; 2 Sam. 14–15; Heb. 3–5
- [ ] 22 Prov. 5; 2 Sam. 16–17; Heb. 6
- [ ] 23 Prov. 6; 2 Sam. 18–19; Heb. 7
- [ ] 24 Prov. 7; 2 Sam. 20–21; Heb. 8
- [ ] 25 Prov. 8; 2 Sam. 22–23; Heb. 9–10
- [ ] 26 Prov. 9; 2 Sam. 24; Heb. 11
- [ ] 27 Prov. 10; 1 Kings 1–3; Heb. 12
- [ ] 28 Prov. 11–12; 1 Kings 4–5; Heb. 13
- [ ] 29 Prov. 13; 1 Kings 6–7; James 1–2
- [ ] 30 Prov. 14; 1 Kings 8–9; James 3
- [ ] 31 Prov. 15; 1 Kings 10–11; James 4–5

June

- [ ] 1 Prov. 16; 1 Kings 12–13; 1 Peter 1
- [ ] 2 Prov. 17; 1 Kings 14–15; 1 Peter 2
- [ ] 3 Prov. 18; 1 Kings 16–17; 1 Peter 3–4
- [ ] 4 Prov. 19–20; 1 Kings 18–19; 1 Peter 5
- [ ] 5 Prov. 21–22; 1 Kings 20; 2 Peter 1
- [ ] 6 Prov. 23; 1 Kings 21–22; 2 Peter 2
- [ ] 7 Prov. 24; 2 Kings 1–3; 2 Peter 3
- [ ] 8 Prov. 25; 2 Kings 4–5; 1 Jn. 1
- [ ] 9 Prov. 26; 2 Kings 6–7; 1 Jn. 2
- [ ] 10 Prov. 27; 2 Kings 8–9; 1 Jn. 3
- [ ] 11 Prov. 28; 2 Kings 10–11; 1 Jn. 4–5
- [ ] 12 Prov. 29; 2 Kings 12–13; 2 John
- [ ] 13 Prov. 30; 2 Kings 14–15; 3 John
- [ ] 14 Prov. 31; 2 Kings 16–17; Jude
- [ ] 15 Eccl. 1; 2 Kings 18–19; Rev. 1
- [ ] 16 Eccl. 2; 2 Kings 20–21; Rev. 2
- [ ] 17 Eccl. 3; 2 Kings 22–23; Rev. 3
- [ ] 18 Eccl. 4; 2 Kings 24–25; Rev. 4
- [ ] 19 Eccl. 5; 1 Chron. 1–2; Rev. 5–7
- [ ] 20 Eccl. 6; 1 Chron. 3–4; Rev. 8

☐ 21 Eccl. 7; 1 Chron. 5–6; Rev. 9

☐ 22 Eccl. 8; 1 Chron. 7–8; Rev. 10

☐ 23 Eccl. 9; 1 Chron. 9–10; Rev. 11

☐ 24 Eccl. 10; 1 Chron. 11–12; Rev. 12

☐ 25 Eccl. 11; 1 Chron. 13–14; Rev. 13

☐ 26 Eccl. 12; 1 Chron. 15–16; Rev. 14–15

☐ 27 S. of S. 1–2; 1 Chron. 17–18; Rev. 16

☐ 28 S. of S. 3–4; 1 Chron. 19–20; Rev. 17

☐ 29 S. of S. 5; 1 Chron. 21–22; Rev. 18

☐ 30 S. of S. 6; 1 Chron. 23–24; Rev. 19

July

☐ 1 S. of S. 7–8; 1 Chron. 25–26; Rev. 20

☐ 2 Ps. 1; 1 Chron. 27–28; Rev. 21–22

☐ 3 Ps. 2; 1 Chron. 29; Mt. 1–3

☐ 4 Ps. 3; 2 Chron. 1–3; Mt. 4

☐ 5 Ps. 4; 2 Chron. 4–5; Mt. 5

☐ 6 Ps. 5; 2 Chron. 6–7; Mt. 6

☐ 7 Ps. 6; 2 Chron. 8–9; Mt. 7–8

☐ 8 Ps. 7; 2 Chron. 10–11; Mt. 9–11

☐ 9 Ps. 8; 2 Chron. 12–13; Mt. 12

☐ 10 Ps. 9; 2 Chron. 14–15; Mt. 13

☑ 11 Ps. 10; 2 Chron. 16–17; Mt. 14

☐ 12 Ps. 11; 2 Chron. 18–19; Mt. 15–16

☐ 13 Ps. 12; 2 Chron. 20–21; Mt. 17

☐ 14 Ps. 13; 2 Chron. 22–23; Mt. 18–20

☐ 15 Ps. 14; 2 Chron. 24–25; Mt. 21

☐ 16 Ps. 15; 2 Chron. 26–27; Mt. 22

☐ 17 Ps. 16; 2 Chron. 28–29; Mt. 23

☐ 18 Ps. 17; 2 Chron. 30–31; Mt. 24–25

☐ 19 Ps. 18; 2 Chron. 32–33; Mt. 26

☐ 20 Ps. 19; 2 Chron. 34–35; Mt. 27–28

☐ 21 Ps. 20; 2 Chron. 36; Mk. 1–2

☐ 22 Ps. 21; Ezra 1–3; Mk. 3

☐ 23 Ps. 22; Ezra 4–5; Mk. 4

☐ 24 Ps. 23; Ezra 6–7; Mk. 5

☐ 25 Ps. 24; Ezra 8–9; Mk. 6–7

☐ 26 Ps. 25; Ezra 10; Mk. 8–10

☐ 27 Ps. 26; Neh. 1–3; Mk. 11

☐ 28 Ps. 27; Neh. 4–5; Mk. 12

☐ 29 Ps. 28; Neh. 6–7; Mk. 13

☐ 30 Ps. 29; Neh. 8–9; Mk. 14

☐ 31 Ps. 30; Neh. 10–11; Mk. 15

August

☐ 1 Ps. 31; Neh. 12–13; Mk. 16

☐ 2 Ps. 32; Esther 1–2; Lk. 1–3

☐ 3 Ps. 33; Esther 3–4; Lk. 4

☐ 4 Ps. 34; Esther 5–6; Lk. 5

☐ 5 Ps. 35; Esther 7–8; Lk. 6–7

☐ 6 Ps. 36; Esther 9–10; Lk. 8

☐ 7 Ps. 37; Job 1–2; Lk. 9

☐ 8 Ps. 38; Job 3–4; Lk. 10–12

☐ 9 Ps. 39; Job 5–6; Lk. 13

☐ 10 Ps. 40; Job 7–8; Lk. 14–15

☐ 11 Ps. 41; Job 9–10; Lk. 16

☐ 12 Ps. 42; Job 11–12; Lk. 17–18

☐ 13 Ps. 43; Job 13–14; Lk. 19

☐ 14 Ps. 44; Job 15–16; Lk. 20–21

☐ 15 Ps. 45; Job 17–18; Lk. 22

☐ 16 Ps. 46; Job 19–20; Lk. 23–24

☐ 17 Ps. 47; Job 21–22; Jn. 1–2

☐ 18 Ps. 48; Job 23–24; Jn. 3

☐ 19 Ps. 49; Job 25–26; Jn. 4–6

☐ 20 Ps. 50; Job 27–28; Jn. 7

☐ 21 Ps. 51; Job 29–30; Jn. 8

☐ 22 Ps. 52; Job 31–32; Jn. 9

☐ 23 Ps. 53; Job 33–34; Jn. 10

☐ 24 Ps. 54; Job 35–36; Jn. 11

☐ 25 Ps. 55; Job 37–38; Jn. 12

☐ 26 Ps. 56; Job 39–40; Jn. 13–15

☐ 27 Ps. 57; Job 41–42; Jn. 16

☐ 28 Ps. 58; Isaiah 1–2; Jn. 17

☐ 29 Ps. 59; Isaiah 3–4; Jn. 18–19
☐ 30 Ps. 60; Isaiah 5–6; Jn. 20
☐ 31 Ps. 61; Isaiah 7–8; Jn. 21

September

☐ 1 Ps. 62; Isaiah 9–10; Acts 1–3
☐ 2 Ps. 63; Isaiah 11–12; Acts 4
☐ 3 Ps. 64; Isaiah 13–14; Acts 5
☐ 4 Ps. 65; Isaiah 15–16; Acts 6
☐ 5 Ps. 66; Isaiah 17–18; Acts 7–8
☐ 6 Ps. 67; Isaiah 19–20; Acts 9
☐ 7 Ps. 68; Isaiah 21–22; Acts 10–12
☐ 8 Ps. 69; Isaiah 23–24; Acts 13
☐ 9 Ps. 70; Isaiah 25–26; Acts 14
☐ 10 Ps. 71; Isaiah 27–28; Acts 15
☐ 11 Ps. 72; Isaiah 29–30; Acts 16
☐ 12 Ps. 73; Isaiah 31–32; Acts 17–18
☐ 13 Ps. 74; Isaiah 33–34; Acts 19–21

☐ 14 Ps. 75; Isaiah 35–36; Acts 22
☐ 15 Ps. 76; Isaiah 37–38; Acts 23
☐ 16 Ps. 77; Isaiah 39–40; Acts 24
☐ 17 Ps. 78; Isaiah 41–42; Acts 25
☐ 18 Ps. 79; Isaiah 43–44; Acts 26–27
☐ 19 Ps. 80; Isaiah 45–46; Acts 28
☐ 20 Ps. 81; Isaiah 47–48; Rom. 1–3
☐ 21 Ps. 82; Isaiah 49–50; Rom. 4
☐ 22 Ps. 83–84; Isaiah 51–52; Rom. 5
☐ 23 Ps. 85; Isaiah 53–54; Rom. 6–7
☐ 24 Ps. 86; Isaiah 55–56; Rom. 8
☐ 25 Ps. 87; Isaiah 57–58; Rom. 9–11
☐ 26 Ps. 88; Isaiah 59–60; Rom. 12
☐ 27 Ps. 89; Isaiah 61–62; Rom. 13
☐ 28 Ps. 90; Isaiah 63–64; Rom. 14–15
☐ 29 Ps. 91; Isaiah 65–66; Rom. 16
☐ 30 Ps. 92; Jer. 1–2; 1 Cor. 1

October

☐ 1 Ps. 93; Jer. 3–4; 1 Cor. 2–4

☐ 2 Ps. 94; Jer. 5–6; 1 Cor. 5

☐ 3 Ps. 95; Jer. 7–8; 1 Cor. 6

☐ 4 Ps. 96; Jer. 9–10; 1 Cor. 7

☐ 5 Ps. 97; Jer. 11–12; 1 Cor. 8–9

☐ 6 Ps. 98; Jer. 13–14; 1 Cor. 10

☐ 7 Ps. 99; Jer. 15–16; 1 Cor. 11–13

☐ 8 Ps. 100; Jer. 17–18; 1 Cor. 14

☐ 9 Ps. 101; Jer. 19–20; 1 Cor. 15

☐ 10 Ps. 102; Jer. 21–22; 1 Cor. 16

☐ 11 Ps. 103; Jer. 23–24; 2 Cor. 1

☐ 12 Ps. 104; Jer. 25–26; 2 Cor. 2–3

☐ 13 Ps. 105; Jer. 27–28; 2 Cor. 4–6

☐ 14 Ps. 106; Jer. 29–30; 2 Cor. 7

☐ 15 Ps. 107; Jer. 31–32; 2 Cor. 8

☐ 16 Ps. 108; Jer. 33–34; 2 Cor. 9

☐ 17 Ps. 109; Jer. 35–36; 2 Cor. 10

☐ 18 Ps. 110; Jer. 37–38; 2 Cor. 11

☐ 19 Ps. 111; Jer. 39–40; 2 Cor. 12–13

☐ 20 Ps. 112; Jer. 41–42; Gal. 1–3

☐ 21 Ps. 113; Jer. 43–44; Gal. 4

☐ 22 Ps. 114; Jer. 45–46; Gal. 5

☐ 23 Ps. 115; Jer. 47–48; Gal. 6

☐ 24 Ps. 116; Jer. 49–50; Eph. 1

☐ 25 Ps. 117; Jer. 51–52; Eph. 2

☐ 26 Ps. 118; Lam. 1–2; Eph. 3–5

☐ 27 Ps. 119:1–48; Lam. 3–4; Eph. 6

☐ 28 Ps. 119:49–80; Lam. 5; Phil. 1

☐ 29 Ps. 119:81–96; Ezek. 1–3; Phil. 2–3

☐ 30 Ps. 119:97–128; Ezek. 4–5; Phil. 4

☐ 31 Ps. 119:129–144; Ezek. 6–7; Col. 1

November

☐ 1 Ps. 119:145–176; Ezek. 8–9; Col. 2–4

☐ 2 Ps. 120; Ezek. 10–11; 1 Thess. 1

☐ 3 Ps. 121; Ezek. 12–13; 1 Thess. 2–3

☐ 4 Ps. 122; Ezek. 14–15; 1 Thess. 4

☐ 5 Ps. 123; Ezek. 16–17; 1 Thess. 5

☐ 6 Ps. 124; Ezek. 18–19; 2 Thess. 1

☐ 7 Ps. 125; Ezek. 20–21; 2 Thess. 2–3

☐ 8 Ps. 126; Ezek. 22–23; 1 Tim. 1–2

☐ 9 Ps. 127; Ezek. 24–25; 1 Tim. 3

☐ 10 Ps. 128; Ezek. 26–27; 1 Tim. 4

☐ 11 Ps. 129–130; Ezek. 28–29; 1 Tim. 5–6

☐ 12 Ps. 131; Ezek. 30–31; 2 Tim. 1–2

☐ 13 Ps. 132; Ezek. 32–33; 2 Tim. 3–4

☐ 14 Ps. 133; Ezek. 34–35; Titus 1

☐ 15 Ps. 134; Ezek. 36–37; Titus 2–3

☐ 16 Ps. 135; Ezek. 38–39; Philemon

☐ 17 Ps. 136; Ezek. 40–41; Heb. 1

☐ 18 Ps. 137; Ezek. 42–43; Heb. 2

☐ 19 Ps. 138; Ezek. 44–45; Heb. 3–5

☐ 20 Ps. 139; Ezek. 46–47; Heb. 6

☐ 21 Ps. 140; Ezek. 48; Heb. 7

☐ 22 Ps. 141; Dan. 1–3; Heb. 8

☐ 23 Ps. 142; Dan. 4–5; Heb. 9–10

☐ 24 Ps. 143; Dan. 6–7; Heb. 11

☐ 25 Ps. 144; Dan. 8–9; Heb. 12

☐ 26 Ps. 145; Dan. 10–11; Heb. 13

☐ 27 Ps. 146; Dan. 12; James 1–2

☐ 28 Ps. 147; Hosea 1–3; James 3

☐ 29 Ps. 148; Hosea 4–5; James 4–5

☐ 30 Ps. 149–150; Hosea 6–7; 1 Peter 1

December

☐ 1 Prov. 1; Hosea 8–9; 1 Peter 2

☐ 2 Prov. 2; Hosea 10–11; 1 Peter 3

☐ 3 Prov. 3; Hosea 12–13; 1 Peter 4–5

☐ 4 Prov. 4; Hosea 14; 2 Peter 1

☐ 5 Prov. 5; Joel 1–3; 2 Peter 2

☐ 6 Prov. 6; Amos 1–2; 2 Peter 3

☐ 7 Prov. 7; Amos 3–4; 1 Jn. 1

☐ 8 Prov. 8; Amos 5–6; 1 Jn. 2

- ☐ 9 Prov. 9; Amos 7–9; 1 Jn. 3
- ☐ 10 Prov. 10; Obadiah; 1 Jn. 4–5
- ☐ 11 Prov. 11; Jonah 1–2; 2 John
- ☐ 12 Prov. 12; Jonah 3–4; 3 John
- ☐ 13 Prov. 13; Micah 1–2; Jude
- ☐ 14 Prov. 14; Micah 3–4; Rev. 1
- ☐ 15 Prov. 15; Micah 5–6; Rev. 2
- ☐ 16 Prov. 16; Micah 7; Rev. 3
- ☐ 17 Prov. 17; Nahum 1–3; Rev. 4
- ☐ 18 Prov. 18; Hab. 1–2; Rev. 5–7
- ☐ 19 Prov. 19; Hab. 3; Rev. 8
- ☐ 20 Prov. 20; Zeph. 1–3; Rev. 9
- ☐ 21 Prov. 21; Hag. 1–2; Rev. 10
- ☐ 22 Prov. 22; Zech. 1–2; Rev. 11
- ☐ 23 Prov. 23; Zech. 3–4; Rev. 12
- ☐ 24 Prov. 24; Zech. 5–6; Rev. 13
- ☐ 25 Prov. 25; Zech. 7–8; Rev. 14–15
- ☐ 26 Prov. 26; Zech. 9–10; Rev. 16
- ☐ 27 Prov. 27; Zech. 11–12; Rev. 17
- ☐ 28 Prov. 28; Zech. 13–14; Rev. 18
- ☐ 29 Prov. 29; Mal. 1–2; Rev. 19
- ☐ 30 Prov. 30; Mal. 3; Rev. 20
- ☐ 31 Prov. 31; Mal. 4; Rev. 21–22

Steps For Personal Prayer

(How to Spend As Much As One Hour Daily in Prayer.)

The following prayer guide will help you spend up to one hour in prayer each day. Remember, Jesus said to one of His disciples, "Could you not watch with Me one hour?" (Matthew 26:40). If you spend just five minutes for each of the twelve aspects of prayer in the circle on page 73, you will devote a full hour to prayer. But don't be legalistic in your daily prayer time. Even one or two minutes in each aspect of prayer will greatly enhance your growth in Jesus. (Please read the Bible verses suggested for each aspect of prayer listed.)

Note: The prayer steps are explained in depth in the book *The Hour that Changes the World* by Dick Eastman.

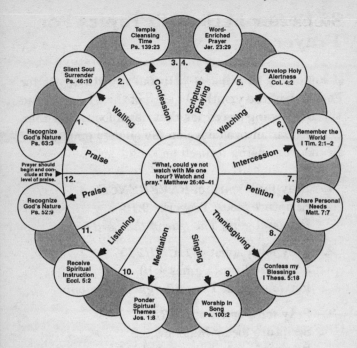

31 Personal Growth Topics For Prayer

Following is a list of personal growth topics for each day of the month. On each of the 31 days, read the Bible verse listed for that day's focus and then ask God to help you develop the quality emphasized in the word being focused on.

1. Pray for a spirit of *REVERENCE*.
   Scripture focus: Proverbs 9:10
   Personal goal: *The fear of the Lord*

2. Pray for a spirit of *HUMILITY*.
   Scripture focus: James 4:10
   Personal goal: *The willingness to submit*

3. Pray for a spirit of *PURITY*.
   Scripture focus: Matthew 5:8
   Personal goal: *A desire to be clean*

4. Pray for a spirit of *PURPOSE*.
   Scripture focus: Proverbs 4:25
   Personal goal: *The wisdom to set goals*

5. Pray for a spirit of *SIMPLICITY*.
   Scripture focus: Romans 12:8
   Personal goal: *A lifestyle uncluttered*

6. Pray for a spirit of *COMMITMENT*.
   Scripture focus: Joshua 24:15
   Personal goal: *Dedication to the cause of Christ*

7. Pray for a spirit of *DILIGENCE*.
   Scripture focus: 2 Peter 1:5
   Personal goal: *The willingness to work hard*

8. Pray for a spirit of *SERVANTHOOD*.
   Scripture focus: Galatians 6:9–10
   Personal goal: *The ministry of helping others*

9. Pray for a spirit of *CONSISTENCY*.
   Scripture focus: James 1:8
   Personal goal: *The quality of faithfulness*

10. Pray for a spirit of *ASSURANCE*.
    Scripture focus: Hebrews 10:22.
    Personal goal: *A depth of faith*

11. Pray for a spirit of *AVAILABILITY*.
    Scripture focus: Isaiah 6:8.
    Personal goal: *A readiness to go*

12. Pray for a spirit of *LOYALTY*.
    Scripture focus: Ruth 1:16
    Personal goal: *A zeal for fidelity*

13. Pray for a spirit of *SENSITIVITY*.
    Scripture focus: Luke 10:30–37
    Personal goal: *Openness of heart*

14. Pray for a spirit of *COMPASSION*.
    Scripture focus: Mark 8:1–2
    Personal goal: *Love in action*

15. Pray for a spirit of *TENDERNESS*.
    Scripture focus: 2 Kings 22:19
    Personal goal: *A willingness to weep*

16. Pray for a spirit of *MATURITY*.
    Scripture focus: Hebrews 5:12–14
    Personal goal: *The capacity to grow*

17. Pray for a spirit of *HOLINESS*.
    Scripture focus: 1 Peter 1:16
    Personal goal: *Christlike behavior*

18. Pray for a spirit of *RELIABILITY*.
    Scripture focus: 1 Corinthians 4:2
    Personal foal: *A depth of dependability*

19. Pray for a spirit of *REVELATION*.
    Scripture focus: Ephesians 1:15–18
    Personal goal: *Learning to listen*

20. Pray for a spirit of *SELF-DENIAL*.
    Scripture focus: Luke 9:23
    Personal goal: *Sacrifice of surrender*

21. Pray for a spirit of *CONFIDENCE*.
    Scripture focus: Philippians 4:13
    Personal goal: *A baptism in boldness*

22. Pray for a spirit of *INTEGRITY*.
    Scripture focus: Romans 12:17
    Personal goal: *The quality of truthfulness*

23. Pray for a spirit of *REPENTANCE*.
    Scripture focus: Luke 3:8
    Personal foal: *A willingness to change*

24. Pray for a spirit of *TRUST*.
    Scripture focus: Psalm 125:1
    Personal goal: *A fearless reliance*

25. Pray for a spirit of *SUBMISSION*.
    Scripture focus: Ephesians 5:21
    Personal goal: *Choosing to yield*

26. Pray for a spirit of *TEACHABILITY*.
    Scripture focus: Titus 3:2
    Personal goal: *The quality of meekness*

27. Pray for a spirit of *PRAYER*.
    Scripture focus: Isaiah 40:31
    Personal goal: *A longing to wait*

28. Pray for a spirit of *UNITY*.
    Scripture focus: 1 Corinthians 1:10
    Personal goal: *A respect for others*

29. Pray for a spirit of *RESTORATION*.
    Scripture focus: Isaiah 61:1–2
    Personal goal: *A ministry of healing*

30. Pray for a spirit of *AUTHORITY*.
    Scripture focus: Matthew 16:19
    Personal goal: *A capacity to command*

31. Pray for a spirit of *GENEROSITY*.
    Scripture focus: Matthew 10:8
    Personal goal: *The desire to give*

Seven Keys to a Better Life

Other books by Dick Eastman:

The Hour that Changes the World—an in-depth
plan to spend up to one hour daily in prayer
The University of the Word—a twelve-step plan to
help you grow in God's Word
Love On Its Knees—a guide to prayer for other
people and lands with Christ as our example

EVERY HOME FOR CHRIST · P.O. Box 7139
Canoga Park, CA 91304

Canada · Australia
P.O. Box 3636 *P.O. Box 168*
Guelph, Ontario *Penshurst*
NIH 7S2 *N.S.W. 2222*

South Africa · United Kingdom
P.O. Box 7086 *71 Clifton Road*
Primrose Hill 1417 *Shefford, Bedfordshire*
Republic of S. Africa *SGI7 5AG*

Personal Growth Response Page

If you have made a personal decision to acknowledge Jesus Christ as Lord of your life, please return this entire page to the address listed on page 78.

☐ Yes, I have received Jesus Christ as my personal Lord and Savior.

Date:_____

☐ I have already made a commitment to receive Jesus Christ as Savior, but I desire to grow more in Him.

☐ Please send me a free copy of your full-color *World Prayer Map* to help me pray for the nations of the world each day.

☐ Please send me information on the books mentioned on the previous page.

NAME_____

ADDRESS_____

CITY_____**STATE**_____**ZIP**_____